3 0063 00318 7731

Main   March 2019

Be a Space Scientist!

EARTH'S NEAREST NEIGHBORS

CAN *YOU* EXPLORE THE INNER PLANETS?

David Hawksett

PowerKiDS press

New York

$$d = \sqrt{(x_2 - x_1) + (y_2 - y_1)^2}$$

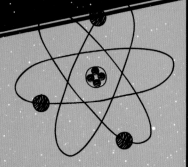

Published in 2018 by **The Rosen Publishing Group, Inc.**
29 East 21st Street, New York, NY 10010

Cataloging-in-Publication Data

Names: Hawksett, David.
Title: Earth's nearest neighbors: can you explore the inner planets? / David Hawksett.
Description: New York : PowerKids Press, 2018. | Series: Be a space scientist! | Includes index.
Identifiers: ISBN 9781538322925 (pbk.) | ISBN 9781538321997 (library bound) | ISBN 9781538322932 (6 pack)
Subjects: LCSH: Inner planets--Juvenile literature.
Classification: LCC QB606.H39 2018 | DDC 523.4--dc23

Copyright © 2018 by The Rosen Publishing Group, Inc.

Produced for Rosen by Calcium
Editors for Calcium: Sarah Eason and Jennifer Sanderson
Designers for Calcium: Paul Myerscough and Jeni Child
Picture Researcher: Rachel Blount

Photo Credits: Cover: NASA/JPL: tl, tc, tr; Shutterstock: Nostalgia for Infinity br; Wikimedia Commons: NASA bl; Inside: NASA: 24–25, NASA/Johns Hopkins University Applied Physics Laboratory/Carnegie Institution of Washington 28–29b, NASA/JPL-Caltech/UCLA/MPS/DLR/IDA 32, 45c; Martin J Powell, www.nakedeyeplanets.com: 9c; Shutterstock: Aleks49 20b, Alexaldo 6–7t, Ralu Cohn 33b, Attila Jandi 15bc, LeonP 15t, 44c, Madlen 33c, Oscity 29, Phloem 33t, Jonathan Pledger 15bl, Kristina Shevchenko 9r, Vectortatu 4, Zwiebackesser 5; Wikimedia Commons: Armael 11, Brocken Inaglory 8, 44t, KillOrDie 22–23t, Jeff Kubina 25b, C. Liefke/ESO 7b, NASA 10–11, 12, 13, 17b, 18, 27r, 40–41, NASA Goddard Space Flight Center 8–9, NASA/JHU/APL 38–39, NASA/Johns Hopkins University Applied Physics Laboratory/Carnegie Institution of Washington 39b, NASA/JPL 14, 30, 31, 35, 36–37, 37t, NASA/JPL-Caltech 42–43, 42l, NASA/JPL/Corby Waste 20–21, 34, 44b, NASA/JPL/USGS 1, 26–27, 41br, 41cr, 45t, 45b, Pioneer Venus Orbiter (NASA) 16–17, NASA, modifications by Seddon 19, Union of Soviet Socialist Republics/Powered by NASA, National Space Science Data Center 22–23b.

All rights reserved. No part of this book may be reproduced in any form without permission in writing from the publisher, except by a reviewer.

Manufactured in China

CPSIA Compliance Information: Batch BW18PK: For Further Information contact Rosen Publishing, New York, New York at 1-800-237-9932.

CONTENTS

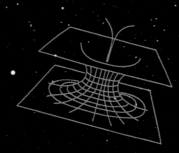

Chapter 1
WORLDS OF ROCK AND FIRE

For thousands of years, people on Earth have gazed up at the stars and our amazing **solar system**. Ancient astronomers used the stars to mark the changing seasons. Earth orbits the sun, and at specific times it blocks our view of certain stars. That is why different stars can be seen at different times during the year. Using this information, ancient people could figure out exactly where the earth was in its yearly cycle. This helped them know when to plant and **harvest** their crops.

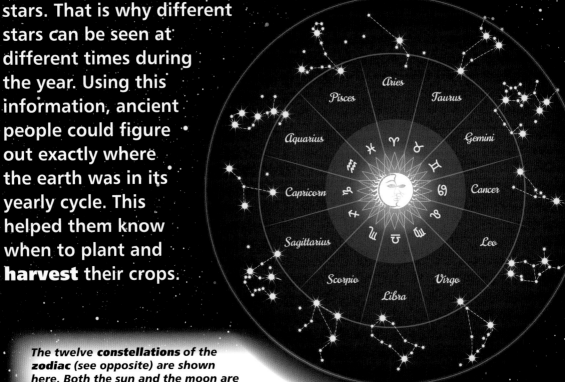

The twelve **constellations** of the **zodiac** (see opposite) are shown here. Both the sun and the moon are shown at the center of the zodiac.

$$d = \sqrt{(x_2 - x_1) + (y_2 - y_1)^2}$$

The Zodiac

The first people to group the stars into constellations were the Sumerians. They lived in an area called Mesopotamia, which is now Iraq. Later, the Babylonians, who also lived in Mesopotamia, charted the stars. They were the first people to realize that the sun passed through the same ring of constellations each year. Today, we call this ring the zodiac.

Measuring Distances in Space

As they watched the sky, ancient people noticed that the sun was not the only object that moved. Five stars also traveled, all at different speeds, but all through the same zodiac constellations as the sun. In around the fourth century BC, the ancient Greeks named these stars *planetes*, which means "wanderer." They also gave them individual names after their gods. At around the same time, the Romans also named the planets after their gods, and it is these names for Mercury, Venus, Mars, and Saturn that we use today.

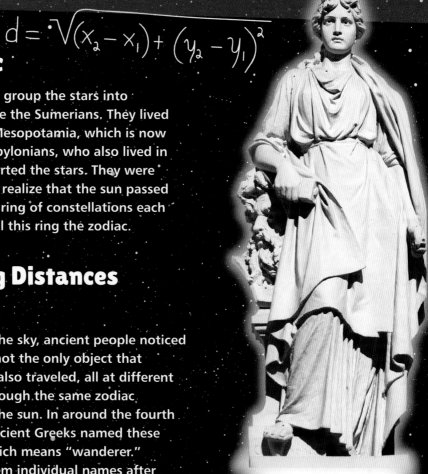

Venus was the Roman goddess of love. She was so important that the Romans named the brightest planet in the night sky after her.

Understanding Our Solar System

Before the late sixteenth century, people believed the stars and planets traveled around Earth. They believed Earth was at the center of the universe. Astronomers who said otherwise were put in prison or even put to death. It was not until the late sixteenth century that people gradually came to accept the idea that Earth and the planets **orbited** the sun. Thanks to **telescopes** and space **probes**, astronomers discovered two additional planets in our solar system: Uranus and Neptune.

THE INNER PLANETS

Jupiter

Earth

Mercury

Venus

Mars

There are two main types of planets that make up our solar system. The first type are big balls of rock. These include Mercury, Venus, Earth, and Mars. They are closest to the sun. These planets make up the inner solar system. They are called the inner planets. The second type are "gas giants," which are planets mostly made of gas. These are Jupiter, Saturn, Uranus, and Neptune. They are far from the sun, in the outer solar system. These planets take longer than the inner planets to orbit the sun. They are known as the outer planets.

Color and Brightness

In the night sky, the inner planets look like bright stars. Mercury is the planet closest to the sun. It is very hard to see, and is only visible just after sunset or just before sunrise. Venus is the next planet, and it shines brightly in the night sky. In fact, after the sun and the moon, it is the brightest natural object in the sky. It can be so bright that it even casts shadows, and is often reported as an Unidentified Flying Object (UFO). If you know exactly where to look, Venus can even be seen in broad daylight. Mars stands out not for its brightness, but its unique color. It is a shade of red.

$$d = \sqrt{(x_2 - x_1) + (y_2 - y_1)^2}$$

This illustration shows the eight major planets of the solar system. Earth is the largest of the four inner rocky planets. Jupiter is the largest of the four outer gas giants.

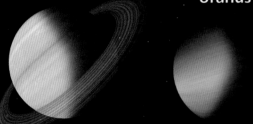

Uranus

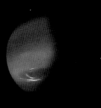

Neptune

Saturn

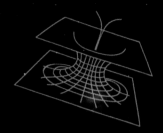

Different Orbits

The changing positions of the planets in the night sky can be explained by their movements. All the planets orbit the sun. It is the sun's **gravity** that keeps the planets locked in orbit around it. If the sun's gravity were turned off, the planets would shoot off into deep space in a straight line. By comparing the movements of the planets, astronomers can tell that Mercury and Venus travel closer to the sun than Earth. Mars is the only inner planet that is farther from the sun than Earth.

Some of the most powerful telescopes are found at the Paranal Observatory in the Atacama Desert in Chile. This image shows ideal conditions to see Mercury. Once it is dark, Mercury will sink below the horizon.

LOOKING AT THE INNER PLANETS

The moon is close enough to Earth for us to be able to see details on its surface without a telescope, but the planets look tiny. However, when you point a telescope at the inner planets, one feature can be seen right away. This is that they show **phases**, like the moon. Phases are changes in a moon's or a planet's shape when seen from Earth. For example, sometimes the moon appears as a crescent and sometimes it appears as a full moon.

Phases are seen because any sphere with a light shone on it will show phases, depending on where the light is. Planets closer to the sun than Earth pass between the sun and Earth during each orbit. When on the same side of the sun as we are, these planets can appear as slim crescents. When Earth and a planet are on opposite sides of the sun, the planet looks more circular.

If you look carefully at this image of the sun, just below the center and slightly to the right is a small black dot. This is Mercury when it passed directly between Earth and the sun in 2006. Events like this are known as transits.

$$d = \sqrt{(x_2 - x_1) + (y_2 - y_1)^2}$$

Be a Space Scientist!

Take a look at these telescope pictures of two of the inner planets. Based on the information below, what do you notice about the planets?

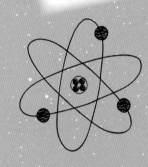

Venus

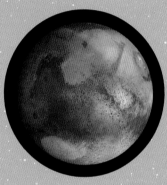

Mars

Mercury

Mercury is visible only during sunrise or sunset, so viewing Mercury through a telescope is difficult. By the time the sky gets dark, Mercury has already fallen below the horizon so it cannot be seen. At sunrise, the brightness of the sky around Mercury drowns out any details.

Venus

Apart from its phase, little of Venus can be seen through a telescope. Venus is covered by swirling clouds, which make it difficult to see anything on the planet's surface.

Mars

Mars is the only inner planet that shows details when seen through a telescope on Earth. The planet has a red color and dark markings that change with the seasons.

Chapter 2
RACE TO THE INNER PLANETS

After World War II (1939–1945), the United States and the United Soviet Socialist Republics (USSR) competed to be the first country to launch machines into space. The USSR sent the first **satellite** into orbit in 1957. However, it was not the satellite that impressed everyone, but the **rocket** that launched it into orbit. To get it there, the rocket had to climb more than 62 miles (100 km) above the ground, which is where space begins. It had to reach a speed of 18,000 miles per hour (28,968 km/h) so the satellite could go all the way around the world in just 96 minutes. Politicians knew such a rocket could also be used to drop bombs anywhere in the world from space, but scientists knew the same rockets could be used to reach the planets.

Built by the National Aeronautics and Space Administration (NASA), the Mercury-Redstone was one of the US's early rockets. It was used on their Mercury Program, which sent the first Americans into space between 1960 and 1961.

Exploring the Solar System

The exploration of the solar system began in 1959, when the USSR launched *Luna 1*. This was a very simple probe designed to smash into the moon. However, a malfunction during launch meant the probe missed the moon entirely and instead went into orbit around the sun. Nicknamed *Mechta*, which means "dream," this tiny probe became the first human-made object to travel beyond the reaches of Earth and the moon.

$$d = \sqrt{(x_2 -}$$

Race to Mars

Next, the inner planets became targets for the **Space Race**. The USSR scored yet another first with the planet Mars when they launched *Mars 2*. This was a much more advanced space probe than *Luna 1* and was launched to Mars in 1971. After a journey of six months, the probe arrived at Mars and sent a **lander** to the surface. During the landing, the parachute failed to open and the lander was destroyed as soon as it touched down. Despite its failure, *Mars 2* became the first human-made object to touch the surface of Mars.

Luna 1 *may have failed to hit the moon, but it did prove that radio communications could successfully travel more than 0.5 million miles (0.8 million km) through space.*

EXPLORING THE INNER PLANETS

$$d = \sqrt{(x_2 - x_1) + (y_2}$$

Most of the early probes to the other worlds in the solar system were simple **flyby** missions. During one of these missions, a rocket blasted off from Earth, carrying a probe. It then gained enough speed to reach the planets in just months. The probe hurtled past the planet at thousands of miles per hour, and took as many pictures and measurements as possible. These were then beamed back to Earth using a radio link.

Earth

Venus

Mercury

Mariner 10 *also encountered Venus on its way to Mercury. It used Venus's gravity to bend its path to allow it to reach Mercury.*

Mercury

Only two spacecraft have ever visited Mercury: *Mariner 10* and *MESSENGER*. *Mariner 10* was the first to see this world up close, in 1974. Its onboard **sensors** revealed that Mercury's surface reached a temperature of 800° F (427 °C), but then dropped to a chilling -297 °F (-183 °C) during the night. Nearly 2,000 photographs were taken and sent back to Earth. They showed that the surface of the planet was covered in **impact craters**. These had been caused by **asteroids** and **comets** hitting the planet over billions of years. *MESSENGER* became the first, and only, probe to orbit Mercury after its arrival in 2011. It mapped the whole planet, including the parts missed by *Mariner 10*. *MESSENGER*'s mission ended in 2015.

Venus

Mariner 2 was the first probe to make a flyby of any planet when it traveled past Venus in 1962. The surface of the planet was invisible because it was completely covered by white clouds. However, *Mariner 2* did discover that the surface of Venus reaches a staggering average temperature of 864 °F (462 °C). This is even hotter than Mercury, which is closer to the sun than Venus!

Mars

Mariner 4 performed the first successful flyby of Mars in 1965. At its closest approach, it passed just 6,000 miles (9,656 km) from the surface of the planet. Its camera snapped 21 pictures of the surface, but the results were disappointing. They showed only impact craters and no **volcanoes**, rivers, or seas to **erode** the craters. These pictures suggested that nothing had happened on Mars's surface for billions of years. This was a major blow for all those people who had hoped to find life on Mars.

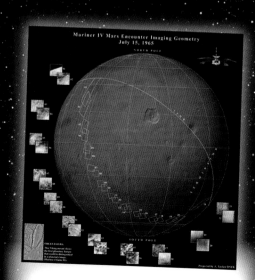

This map of Mars shows what pictures were taken during Mariner 4's *flyby. Each box on the planet represents a*

PROBLEMS WITH FLYBYS

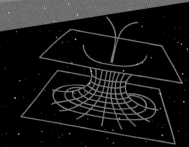

When *Mariner 4* flew by Mars and snapped those first images, it was limited by the technology available in the 1960s. *Mariner 4* had to use an old-fashioned device called a **tape recorder** and could snap only 21 pictures plus a part of another one. Today, a probe flying by Mars would be able to take many thousands of images and record other **data**.

Finding Craters

Apart from confirming the existence of a thin **atmosphere**, the probe only discovered craters. We now know Mars has many other interesting surface features, so why did *Mariner 4* find only craters?

This Mariner 4 *image of Mars shows a large crater 105 miles (169 km) across with smaller craters around it and inside it. We know that the biggest crater is older than the smaller ones inside it, because the big crater would have destroyed the smaller ones if it had been created later.*

$$d = \sqrt{(x_2 - x_1) + (y_2 - y_1)^2}$$

Be a Space Scientist!

Imagine we are going to perform our own flyby. Our own bodies will be the space probe, and our eyes will be the probe's camera. Instead of flying by a planet, we are going to imagine flying past an object on Earth.

Imagine you have never seen an elephant. Then, imagine being *Mariner 4* flying past "planet elephant." You are allowed to take 21 pictures that are all in the same straight line. For planet elephant, our pictures will be around the same size as your hand pressed up against the elephant. Our straight line of photographs can cover only around one-quarter of the width of the elephant. This means you cannot take close-ups of the tail and the trunk during the same flyby.

Now consider how much you could find out about an elephant from these few images. What details do you think might be missing? Could you learn all you need to know about an elephant from just these few photos? How do you think similar challenges make it hard for space scientists to learn all they need to know about a planet? *Mariner 4* was only able to take a few photos of Mars as it flew by. It could photograph only a fraction of the planet's surface, and we now know there was a lot more to learn about Mars.

Compare these two photographs (left) to the one of the elephant shown above. What key information can you learn about the elephant from the top image that is missing in the two images shown left?

Chapter 3
PROBING FOR ANSWERS

Flyby missions are usually the first type of mission to another planet. This means they are our first detailed view of these other worlds. However, flyby missions are basic, with just one chance to discover interesting features. As probes rush past planets in just a few hours, they take photographs of one side of the planet only. A flyby mission to Earth could discover the United States, or Australia, but not both. To find out the true nature of a planet, a probe must get into orbit around that planet.

Slow Down!

When a probe passes a planet, the planet's gravity bends the probe's path, pulling it inward. If the probe brakes hard while this is happening, it slows down enough to be pulled into orbit around the planet. Then, instead of having just one chance to spot things, the probe circles the planet again and again. It can then take images of the whole planet in much more detail.

*In **ultraviolet (UV)** light, structures in Venus's clouds are obvious. However, even UV light is not enough to see through the thick clouds to the planet's surface.*

$$d = \sqrt{(x_2 - x_1) + (y_2 - y_1)^2}$$

Orbiters

NASA's *Pioneer* **orbiter** arrived at Venus in December 1978. The probe had its own rocket engine, so it was able to slow down and enter orbit, becoming a satellite of Venus. *Pioneer* spent nearly 14 years studying Venus. It also sent small probes into Venus's atmosphere, one of which survived for more than one hour on the surface. *Pioneer* measured the planet's winds at 220 miles per hour (354 km/h) at the cloud tops. Today, the temperature on Venus is far too hot for water, but results from *Pioneer* suggest that it once had huge oceans. We still do not know what happened to them.

Two identical probes named *Viking 1* and *Viking 2* entered orbit around Mars in 1976. They studied the planet for four years and six years, respectively, before malfunctioning. They even sent landers to study the planet's surface.

This is one of the landers sent to Mars's surface by the Vikings. The images sent back from a previous spacecraft allowed scientists to choose interesting parts of Mars on which to land.

MARINER 9

The success of the Viking program was due partly to several Mariner missions that had occurred earlier. *Mariner 4* sent back pictures just of craters, but the mission was still a huge achievement for the United States. It was followed up by *Mariner 6* and *Mariner 7*, which were launched in 1969. Both *Mariner 6* and *7* performed a flyby of Mars, but still failed to discover anything interesting. Two years later, in 1971, *Mariner 8* and *Mariner 9* were launched to Mars.

Race to Mars

Mariner 8 malfunctioned on launch and landed in the Atlantic Ocean. However, *Mariner 9* reached Mars in November 1971. It became the first spacecraft ever to orbit another planet, narrowly beating the USSR's *Mars 2* and *Mars 3* probes. Upon arrival, though, Mars was covered in the largest dust storm even seen in the solar system. Both *Mars 2* and *Mars 3* wasted much of their resources snapping shots of the dust. Luckily, NASA was able to reprogram *Mariner 9* to stop working until the dust had settled. Then, after a couple of months, *Mariner 9* went to work.

These images of Mars were both taken by the Hubble Space Telescope. The left one shows surface features including large craters, dark markings, and polar caps. On the right, the whole planet is shrouded in a dust storm.

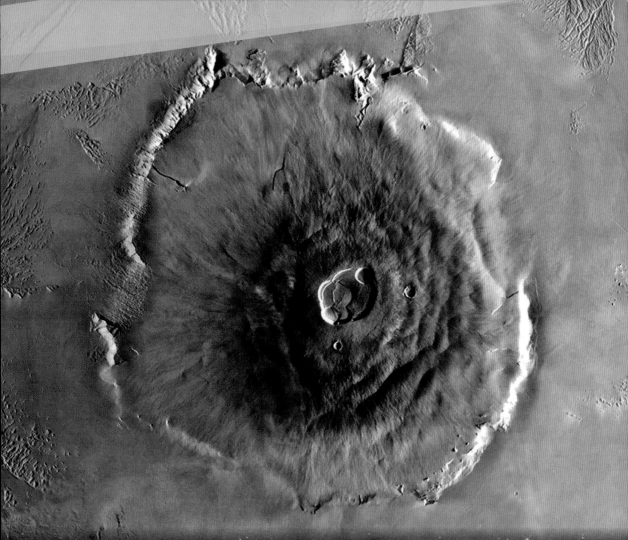

Not Just Craters

Mariner 9 saw the craters from earlier missions, but also found much more. Giant volcanoes, bigger than anything on Earth, were seen on Mars. These were so tall that the **summits** almost touched space! The biggest, Olympus Mons, was about the same size as France! A giant **canyon**, stretching one-quarter of the way around the planet, was named Mariner Valley, after the spacecraft. Perhaps most exciting was the discovery of dried-up river valleys and evidence of enormous flooding across the planet long ago. Mars had become one of the most fascinating places in the solar system.

Olympus Mons measures 370 miles (595 km) across. Its shape shows that it is a shield volcano, much like those that formed the Hawaiian Islands.

$$d = \sqrt{(x_2 - x_1) + (y_2 - y}$$

LANDING ON VENUS

Venus may be named for the Roman goddess of love, but there is nothing lovely about its surface conditions. Data gathered by flyby missions, such as *Mariner 2* and *Mariner 5*, revealed the temperature on the surface to be 864 °F (462 °C). This is hot enough to melt lead. Also, the air on Venus is made almost completely of toxic **carbon dioxide**.

If Venus's temperature and carbon dioxide are not enough to scare you away, its atmosphere may well be. It is around 100 times thicker than Earth's. The air **pressure** on the surface of Venus would make it feel like being 3,000 feet (914 m) deep in the ocean. This thick air is filled with white clouds that look beautiful but are actually deadly. Instead of containing water vapor like Earth's clouds, they are made from **sulfuric acid. Acid rain** falls from the clouds but never reaches the ground. Instead, it **evaporates** in the heat closer to the surface and goes back into the clouds.

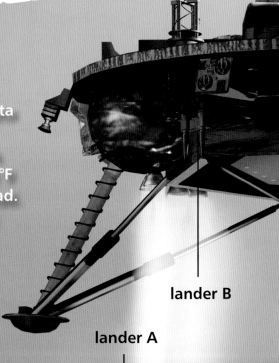

lander B

lander A

The USSR built this lander. Compare this lander to the other one shown above. How is it different?

Be a Space Scientist!

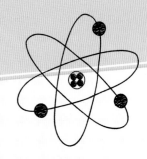

Take a look at the two landers shown on these pages. Can you figure out which planet each lander went to? Remember that the pressure on Venus is intense. Any lander sent there would need to be solidly built and very tough to survive that pressure. Landers designed for Mars only have to cope with a very thin atmosphere. Therefore, their design does not need to be as solid and tough to withstand the atmosphere there.

You can see this lander's rockets firing and its landing legs extended. The probe has scientific instruments and the two spheres on either side of its underside are fuel tanks for its landing rockets.

Designing a Spacecraft

Designing a spacecraft to visit a planet like Venus is complicated. The craft has to be able to travel to the planet in one piece. Then it has to gather the right information and send it back to Earth. If you want to land a probe on a planet, the probe has to be able to survive the conditions there. Venus presented a lot of challenges for space scientists, including some they had not dealt with before. Probes to the moon had to be designed to deal with extremes of temperature between sunlight and shade, but they did not have a **hostile** atmosphere to deal with, too.

Chapter 4
LANDERS

While the United States was the most successful country at landing on Mars, the USSR has achieved the most on Venus. *Venera 3* arrived at Venus in March 1966. Unfortunately, its communications with Earth had failed during the journey, so the probe sent no pictures or data. It entered the atmosphere and almost certainly crash-landed, making it the first probe to crash onto another planet. In 1967, *Venera 4* entered the atmosphere and transmitted data until contact was lost during the probe's **descent** to Venus's surface. The probe was probably crushed by the planet's pressure.

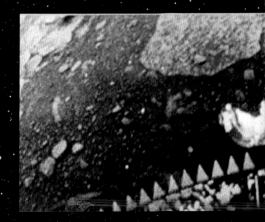

Surviving Venus

In 1970, *Venera 7* made it all the way to Venus's surface. Its parachute failed just before landing, but the probe still survived, toppling onto its side on the surface. It sent back data for 23 minutes before its battery died. *Venera 9* was an orbiter-lander combination. In 1975, this lander survived 52 minutes on the surface and sent back the very first picture of rocks on the ground.

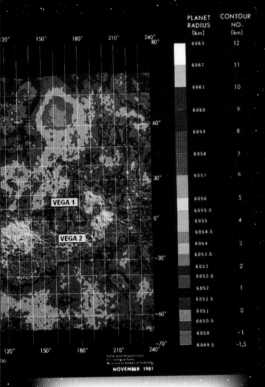

PLANET RADIUS (km)	CONTOUR NO. (km)
6063	12
6062	11
6061	10
6060	9
6059	8
6058	7
6057	6
6056	5
6055.5	
6055	4
6054.5	
6054	3
6053.5	
6053	2
6052.5	
6052	1
6051.5	
6051	0
6050.5	
6050	-1
6049.5	-1.5

N.A.S.A.-Ames Research Center
U.S. Geological Survey
Massachusetts Institute of Technology
NOVEMBER 1981

*This is a **topographic map** of Venus. The lowest areas are in blue and the highest in red and brown. The large yellow area near the top is Aphrodite Terra and is similar to a continent on Earth. The red dots show where Soviet probes have landed.*

$$d = \sqrt{(x_2 - x_1) + (y_6 - y_4)^2}$$

Venus Melts Cameras!

Overall, the Venera probes were a highly successful set of missions. The harsh surface of Venus, however, made their missions very tough. None of the landers lasted more than 127 minutes before the planet's high temperature and pressure destroyed them. During landing, cameras on the probes were protected by lens caps. Once the probes had landed, the lens caps were supposed to be **ejected.** However, some of the caps just melted onto the camera in the heat and no pictures were taken at all.

What Did the Probes See?

The Venera Program did send back pictures. *Venera 13* was the first probe to beam back color pictures of the landscape. They showed a surface of shattered slabs of rock, which was probably volcanic. The sky was a deep orange, and the planet's thick clouds stopped most of the sunlight from reaching the surface. No probes have landed in this hostile place since the 1980s, so our most recent knowledge of the surface is more than 30 years old.

This is the view of the surface of Venus from Venera 13. The camera on the lander is pointing down at the surface in a fish-eye style view. Parts of the lander are seen in the foreground, including an ejected lens cap.

LANDERS ON MARS

More than half of the dozens of missions sent to Mars have failed. Because of this, NASA scientists have jokingly created a space monster named the Great Galactic Ghoul. They say it lies in wait for its favorite snacks: Mars probes!

Great Galactic Ghoul

Of the missions to Mars, the USSR's *Mars 2* and *Mars 3* probes of 1971 both failed. *Mars 3* was able to transmit a tiny part of its first picture before contact was lost just 14.5 seconds after touchdown. The *Mars 6* and *Mars 7* landers, two years later, both failed. One of them even missed the planet by 800 miles (1,287 km). More recently in 1999, NASA's *Mars Polar Lander* crashed instead of landing. The same thing happened to the European Space Agency's (ESA) *Beagle 2* lander in 2003.

Viking 1 was launched from Cape Canaveral in Florida on August 20, 1975. It took 10 months to reach Mars, where it entered orbit instead of flying by once. It consisted of an orbiter and a lander, and was one of the most complex planetary missions.

24

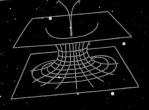

The Vikings

The Viking landers were the first probes to perform a soft landing using parachutes and then rockets to slow down. They were both carried to Mars by the twin Viking orbiters. The landers themselves were big. Each weighed more than 1,200 pounds (544 kg) and carried a range of scientific instruments. These included camera, a **seismometer** to find **marsquakes**, weather sensors, and equipment to study the soil.

Finding Life on Mars?

By the time the Viking landers arrived on Mars, scientists knew there was little chance of finding advanced life. Although no cities or forests were seen from orbit, they hoped there might be **microbes**, or germs. A robotic arm was used to scoop up soil from the surface of Mars and drop it into a sealed container on the lander. The soil **samples** were heated and gave off gas. The results of studying the gas are still uncertain. Some scientists believe today that the Viking experiments do indeed show signs of microbes in the soil.

Both Viking landers carried a robotic arm with a small scoop on the end. Here it is seen practicing on Earth. The arm dug two trenches in the first serious attempt to find life on Mars.

$$d = \sqrt{(x_2 - x_1)^2 + (y_2 - y_1)^2}$$

VENUS FROM ORBIT

On May 4, 1989, NASA's **Space Shuttle** *Atlantis* blasted off from Cape Canaveral in Florida. It was the first shuttle launch to carry an interplanetary spacecraft. Once the cargo bay doors opened, the *Magellan* probe was released. It then fired its own engines to take it to Venus. Like other probes, *Magellan* carried scientific instruments to study the planet from orbit. *Magellan* was the first interplanetary launch for the United States in 11 years and the country's fifth successful Venus mission.

Magellan

Magellan spent more than four years orbiting Venus until it burned up in the atmosphere. It was one of the most successful planetary missions of all time and produced a detailed map of the planet. The topographical map shown above shows the whole of Venus. The blue areas are not oceans — they are the lowest points on Venus. The brown areas show the highest mountains. If Venus had oceans like Earth, they would fill the blue areas, leaving the mountainous regions above water like Earth's continents.

$$d = \sqrt{(x_2 - x_1) + \left(y_2 - y_1\right)^2}$$

Be a Space Scientist!

Look at the *Magellan* spacecraft on the right. Something onboard allowed it to measure distances on Venus to map the planet. Read the information in the "How to Map Venus?" section below. What piece of equipment can you see on the spacecraft that was used to map Venus?

Left: This topographical map shows Venus's high and low points.

Right: The bottom part of Magellan is its rocket engine which was used after it undocked from Atlantis. On top are its scientific instruments.

solar panel   radar dish

USA

rocket engine

How to Map Venus?

Telescopes had shown Venus had a thick atmosphere even before space probes arrived. The sulfuric acid clouds cover 100% of the surface, without even the smallest gap being seen. Radar is a system that works on radio waves bouncing off things to see how far away they are. To map Venus, *Magellan* used radar to measure the distances to the tops of the mountains and the bottoms of the trenches.

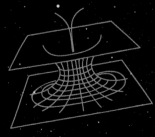

Chapter 5
A CLOSER LOOK

When we look at the surfaces of other planets, we compare them to features we see on Earth. However, there is one type of feature we see more often on Mercury, Mars, and the moon than we see on Earth. All of these bodies are riddled with round depressions called craters.

What Made the Craters?

For years, many scientists believed the craters on the moon, Mercury, and Mars were volcanoes. On Earth, many volcanoes have a crater at the top, often caused when volcanoes erupt. It was not until the 1960s that we realized something else caused the craters on the moon, Mercury, and Mars. In 1960, a young **geologist** named Eugene Shoemaker had studied the famous Barringer Crater in Arizona. He compared it with the craters left behind after **nuclear weapons** were tested, noting that there were similarities. From his work, space scientists concluded that the craters on the moon, Mercury, and Mars were not volcanoes. Instead, they were craters formed by asteroids and comets smashing into the bodies' surfaces at incredibly high speeds.

The Violent Solar System

Asteroids and comets are made up of dust and rocks that were left behind when the planets formed 4.5 billion years ago. The planets and their moons have been gradually sweeping up this **debris** ever since. Whenever an asteroid or comet hit planets like Earth, the planet swallowed up its dust and rock. The planet then grew. It is this process that has helped the planets of our solar system reach their current sizes.

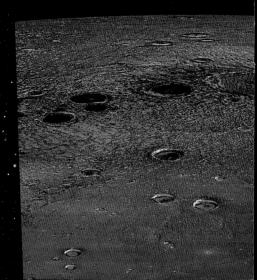

$$d = \sqrt{(x_2 - x_1)^2 + (y_2 - y_1)^2}$$

Barringer Crater near Flagstaff, Arizona, was the first feature on Earth to be identified as an impact crater. It was formed around 50,000 years ago by a rock from space weighing around 300,000 tons (272,155.4 metric tons).

Clues from Craters

Impact craters come in all sizes. Each was caused by a bombardment of objects from space. Each impact creates a huge amount of energy and heat. This can melt the rock around the impact site. The craters left behind can provide clues to what the surface is made of. Some craters on Mars show patterns of low hills around them, which look like mud flows. Scientists believe these craters, called splosh craters, melted ice underground. The ice mixed with rock to make mud, which flowed outward, before freezing again as it cooled down.

This MESSENGER image of Mercury's north polar region shows its craters. It shows the temperature range on Mercury. The red parts are the warmest and the blue parts are the coldest.

29

VOLCANOES

When the planets first formed, they were very hot. Every time an asteroid hit the surface of the planets, they became even hotter. The inner planets were so hot when they first formed that their surfaces were covered in molten (melted) **lava**. Eventually, the planets cooled enough for the surfaces to solidify, or become solid. As they are so big, planets take a long time to cool down. Although they have cooled down enough for their surfaces to become solid, their centers, or cores, are still cooling down today.

$$d = \sqrt{(x_2 - x_1) + (y}$$

This image made using Magellan data shows the volcano Maat Mons on Venus. Maat Mons is the second tallest mountain on Venus and the tallest volcano. Old lava flows can be seen along its right edge, showing up as dark streaks.

Three volcanoes on Mars can be seen
in this image from the Viking 1 orbiter.
The volcanoes are called Ascraeus
Mons, Pavonis Mons, and Arsia Mons.

On Earth

Volcanoes help planets cool down.
When volcanoes erupt, they bring very
hot molten rock from deep below the
surface to the open air, where it can
cool down quickly. Earth is the most
volcanically active world in the inner solar system. It has around
1,500 volcanoes that have erupted in the last 10,000 years. At any
one time, around 20 volcanoes are erupting around the world.

On Mars

When *Mariner 9* discovered volcanoes on Mars, the surprise was the enormous
size of them. Olympus Mons is the biggest mountain in the solar system. Its
summit is 2.5 times the height of the top of Mount Everest, the tallest mountain
on Earth. Even more impressive is that this volcano is on a planet only half the size
of Earth. The clouds that form at its summit can even be seen from Earth through
telescopes. None of the Martian volcanoes are believed to have erupted in the last
few million years or so.

On Venus

Venus has around 1,600 volcanoes, and its surface is almost entirely covered with
a volcanic rock called basalt. No one knew if any of the volcanoes were active until
2015, when Europe's *Venus Express* probe spotted **infrared** heat flashes from an
area near two volcanoes called Maat Mons and Ozzi Mons. The best explanation
for these hot spots is that molten lava or hot volcanic gases are escaping from a
volcanic vent. This proves that volcanoes are still active on Venus.

IMPACT CRATERS

When we look at the surface of Earth, we can identify several main processes that have shaped it. These include volcanic activity, **plate tectonics**, and **erosion**.

Shaping Earth

Volcanoes erupt and grow, covering the land with lava flows and ash. Plate tectonics involves the continental plates under Earth's surface, which shift very slowly. You can see the effect of their movement if you look at the shapes of the West African coast and the South American east coast. They fit together like pieces of a puzzle because they used to be in the same place. Erosion is when the shape of the landscape is gradually worn away. On Earth, water does most of this work, carving rivers and eroding cliffs. While some planets, such as Venus and Mars, have these "surface shapers" in common with Earth, all planets have craters. These craters have shaped the surface of every single planet, moon, and asteroid in the solar system. Let's make a model of an impact crater to show how craters are formed.

This crater, named Haulani, is on the dwarf planet Ceres. It is the largest body in the a "belt" of asteroids between Mars and Jupiter.

$$d = \sqrt{(x_2 - x_1) + (y_2 - y_1)^2}$$

Be a Space Scientist!

You Will Need
- 1 small plastic container, like an empty ice cream container
- All-purpose flour
- Cocoa powder
- 1 marble around the size of a quarter
- An adult

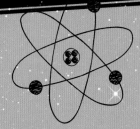

all-purpose flour

Instructions

1. Fill the container with the flour to make the planet's surface.

2. Sprinkle a thin layer of cocoa on top of the flour. This will be a layer of the surface that has been buried.

3. Add another layer of flour so the cocoa is hidden. This top layer could be a lava flow, which has buried the older cocoa landscape as it flowed over it and it became solid.

4. Your marble is the asteroid. Drop it onto the planet's surface from a short distance. Next, ask an adult to help you drop it onto the planet from at least several feet. Ask the adult to drop the asteroid from the top of a stepladder. The higher the drop, the faster and harder the asteroid hits. What happens when the asteroid impacts the surface? Did you expose the hidden layer of cocoa?

cocoa powder

marble

Chapter 6
MODERN EXPLORATION

The probes sent on the early missions to the planets were simple. Although they had few parts that could break and ruin a whole mission, they did have to survive the violent shaking of a rocket launch and then years in space. Onboard computers, containing instructions for the probes, also had to be uncomplicated and shielded against **radiation** from the sun.

Mars Odyssey has been orbiting Mars since October 2001. It has survived longer than any other spacecraft orbiting another planet. It studies Mars and acts as a communications link between Earth and rovers on the Martian surface.

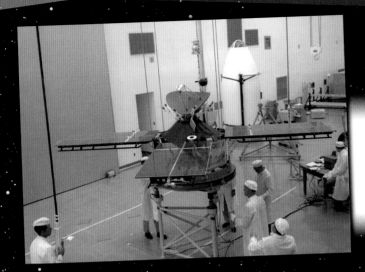

Scientists weigh Mariner 4 before sealing it into its launcher rocket. The weight of a spacecraft helps scientists figure out how much fuel it needs to reach its target.

Better Computers

The *Mariner 4* mission to Mars sent back just 634 kilobytes (KB) of data. A modern smartphone can hold around 128 gigabytes (GB), which is 128,000 KB of data. The phone could hold the data from more than 200,000 *Mariner 4* missions before its memory was full! When the Apollo missions first sent men to the moon in 1969, the onboard guidance computer had a memory of just 64 KB. This is no more powerful than a pocket calculator.

Today, complicated and sophisticated computers power our spacecraft. *Mars Reconnaissance Orbiter* is a NASA mission that arrived at Mars in March 2006. Its onboard memory is split into 700 separate memory chips, each of which can store 256 megabytes (MB) of information. This adds up to around 20 GB, enough to store the data from 33,000 *Mariner 4s*. A single picture of Mars taken by this spacecraft can be as large as 3.5 GB!

A New Kind of Camera

Taking pictures of the planets during the early missions was tricky. The Lunar Orbiter missions took actual photographs, which were developed onboard from negatives. A television camera then scanned the developed pictures and beamed the television signal back to Earth. Modern spacecraft use a technology called charged couple devices, or CCDs. These are digital sensors that take a picture and instantly convert it digital data. They have no moving parts and do not have to develop the picture on the spacecraft. They are the same kind of technology used in today's digital cameras and smartphone cameras.

$d = \sqrt{(x_2 - x_1) + (y_2 - y_1)}$

MARS ROVERS

Landers stay in one place and use their robotic arms to sample things within reach. Rovers are landers on wheels that can be instructed to go to rocks and other features that scientists want to study. The Soviet *Mars 2* and *Mars 3* missions in 1971 each carried a small rover attached to a cable, but neither mission succeeded. Astronomers had to wait until 1997 to drive on Mars.

Pathfinder

Mars Pathfinder landed in Ares Valles on Mars on July 4, 1997. It brought with it a small rover named *Sojourner*. This six-wheeled robot was the size of a microwave oven and could travel at 0.4 inch per second (1 cm/s). It spent three months studying rocks near its mother ship.

The ultimate selfie! NASA's Curiosity rover uses the camera on its robot arm to take a picture of itself. You can see its main camera on the top left and tracks left in the Martian soil in Gale Crater.

$$d = \sqrt{(x_2 - x_1) + (y_}$$

Sojourner *used a solar panel to provide its power. It was too small to contain an antenna strong enough communicate with Earth and so used the* Pathfinder *lander to send and receive messages.*

Spirit and Opportunity

The next rovers were NASA's *Spirit* and *Opportunity*, which landed on Mars in January 2004. They were bigger than *Sojourner*, around 5.2 feet (1.6 m) long, and weighed 400 pounds (181 kg). Both *Spirit* and *Opportunity* rovers had **transmitters** powerful enough to communicate with computers on Earth. This means they could go as far as mission controllers wanted them to travel. In February 2017, *Opportunity* was still working, having traveled more than 27 miles (43 km) across Mars.

Curiosity

The latest rover, *Curiosity*, is the size of a small car. It landed on Mars in August 2012, and is currently exploring Gale Crater, which scientists believe used to contain a shallow sea. It has cameras and a laser to analyze rock chemistry. Its other instruments include a drill to take samples from Mars rocks and a microscope. It can travel at 295 feet per hour (90 m/h) and uses **artificial intelligence** to automatically avoid big rocks or steep slopes that could wreck it.

EXPLORING MERCURY AND VENUS

During the twentieth century, only one mission was sent to the innermost planet, Mercury. *Mariner 10* was successful but performed only flybys and could not take pictures of the whole planet. The ESA was successful in its first mission to j48 with *Venus Express*. Arriving in Venus's orbit in April 2006, *Venus Express* studied the planet for nearly 10 years before burning up as it entered Venus's atmosphere.

MESSENGER

The first Mercury mission to enter orbit was *MESSENGER*. It entered Mercury's orbit in 2011 and mapped the entire surface in great detail. Its orbit gradually decayed until it crashed onto the planet's surface in April 2015. One of its most exciting discoveries lay in the shadows deep within craters at Mercury's north pole. With no atmosphere and scorching temperatures, Mercury is the last place you would expect to find ice. However, *MESSENGER* found ice in the places where sunlight never reaches.

Solar power is readily available at Mercury, but orbiting a planet this close to the sun is hazardous. The sun's heat could destroy the onboard instruments so **MESSENGER** *included a sunshade to keep its instruments out of direct sunlight.*

Venus Express

NASA's *Magellan* mission had produced maps of Venus's surface using radar, so *Venus Express* focused on the planet's atmosphere. It found that more lightning strikes happen on Venus than on Earth. It also found an **ozone layer**, a bit like Earth's, high above the surface. Even though the temperature on the ground is hot enough to melt lead, there are much cooler parts higher up. *Venus Express* found a layer in the atmosphere where carbon dioxide probably falls as snow.

Japanese Missions

In contrast to the ESA's first mission to Venus, the Japan Aerospace Exploration Agency (JAXA) did not have a good start to its missions. JAXA's first mission to Venus failed to enter orbit in December 2010 and spent five years orbiting the sun. Mission controllers performed careful firings of its rocket thrusters and finally got the probe into Venus's orbit in December 2015. One of its discoveries so far was a sideways-smile-shaped feature in the atmosphere. Stretching 6,000 miles (9,656 km), almost from pole to pole, this smile shape lasted four days. It was probably caused by air passing over a mountain region the size of Africa.

$$d = \sqrt{(x_2 - x_1) + (y_2 - y_1)^2}$$

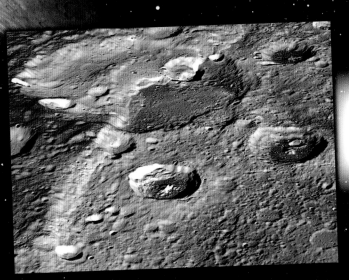

This view of Mercury's surface from **MESSENGER** uses false colors to create a topographic map. Blue shows the lowest points and red-brown the highest.

$$d = \sqrt{(x_2 - x_1) + (y_2 - y_1)^2}$$

CLUES ON THE SURFACE

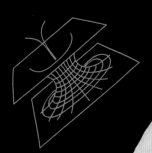

You can learn a lot about a planet just by looking at its surface features. Volcanoes show the planet is or has been geologically active. Wrinkles on Mercury show the planet has shrunk over time in the same way the skin of an apple wrinkles as it dries and shrinks. Very steep cliffs and mountains show that the rock is hard instead of soft. A mountain made of dust would quickly collapse and spread out over the land. Liquid like water on the surface shows the planet must have an atmosphere, otherwise the water would evaporate.

Bombarding Earth

Impact craters occur all over the solar system. Fewer impacts happen today because most of the chunks of rock that cause impact craters have already been swept up by the planets and their moons. Today, thousands of very small rocks hit Earth and land as **meteorites**. Occasionally something bigger hits our planet. In 2013, an asteroid the size of a six-story building exploded in the atmosphere above Russia. The energy released was 33 times that of the atom bomb dropped on Hiroshima, Japan, during World War II in 1945. Nearly 1,500 people were injured and more than 7,000 buildings were damaged.

*This picture of the moon was taken by an astronaut on board Apollo 16, which went to the moon in 1972. It shows regions of the **far side of the moon**, the side that never points toward Earth.*

What We Learn from Craters

Craters may seem boring, but they can be used to learn about the history of a planet or moon. The more craters a surface has, the older it is. A lava flow or erosion will cover up craters or erase them. If an area has few craters, it can be as sign that it is a place that has seen a lot of geological activity, such as volcanic eruptions. Let's examine the photographs of Mars below to find out what they tell us about the two regions.

Be a Space Scientist!

What can we learn from the craters in these pictures? Remember that impacts are just one of the main processes that shape a planet's surface. How many craters can you see in the Amazonis region of Mars compared the Sinus Sabeus region of Mars? Remember what you learned on this page about volcanic activity and how that affects the craters on the surface of a planet. How do you think that might explain why there are different numbers of craters in these two areas of Mars?

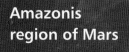

Amazonis region of Mars

Sinus Sabeus region of Mars

THE FUTURE

To study planets' rocks in a state-of-the-art laboratory on Earth, we need **sample-return missions**. These missions have a robot lander scoop up samples of rocks and soil and then blast back off into space to bring them home to Earth.

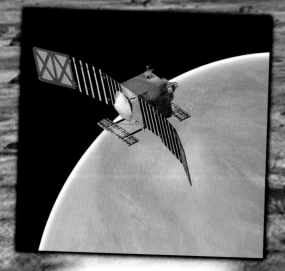

The VERITAS mission was a proposal for a return to Venus by NASA. One of its main goals was to find out if Venus ever had oceans.

More Mars

The only rock samples from other worlds we have were brought back from the moon by astronauts and by the USSR's Luna robots. Probes have also returned dust from a comet and an asteroid. Some meteorites found on Earth are known to be from Mars, but fresh samples would be better. Mars will be the first target for planetary sample-return missions. China plans to do this by 2030, and NASA is currently studying possible mission designs. Between 2018 and 2020, NASA, Europe, Russia, China, India, and the United Arab Emirates (UAE) will all launch robot missions to Mars.

$$d = \sqrt{(x_2 - x_1) + (y_2 - y_1)^2}$$

Neglected Mercury

The BepiColombo mission is set to launch October 2018 and is a joint European-Japanese mission to orbit Mercury. One of its main goals is to further study the water ice found by *MESSENGER* at Mercury's north pole. The only other mission to Mercury is a proposal by Russia to land on the surface. We will have to wait until 2031 before it launches!

Flying on Venus

Russia plans to return to Venus in 2024 with an orbiter and lander that can last longer than a few hours on the surface. There are ideas for missions to Venus that will use robot aircraft that can stay high up in the atmosphere where the temperature is cooler than at the surface.

Mars rovers have given us far more data than we would have gathered using ordinary landers. The next step is to take to the skies. Small robotic helicopters could provide much more detailed photographs of our solar system and allow us to learn even more about it.

BE A SPACE SCIENTIST! ANSWERS

Pages 8–9 Looking at the Inner Planets

You can only see part of Venus. It is shown as a crescent because of its phase. The planet is also covered in clouds, which keep you from seeing any features on its surface. Mars is red in color and has dark markings, which are a result of the dust that blows across the planet's surface.

Pages 14–15 Problems with Flybys

From looking at the top image, you learn that the elephant has four legs, a body, a tail, and a trunk. All of this key information is missing from the two images shown bottom. If the elephant was a planet, much of the important information about it would not be learned from similar flyby images.

Pages 20–21 Landing on Venus

Lander A is solidly built. This lander was built to withstand the pressure on Venus and was the lander sent to that planet. Lander B has spindly legs and fragile parts. This lander was suitable for landing on Mars, but would not have survived the pressure on Venus.

Pages 26–27 Venus from Orbit

Did you spot the radar equipment at the top of *Magellan*? The big dish was used to measure height and depth on Venus. The map of Venus was made using this data.

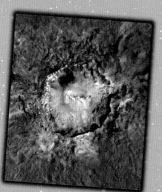

Pages 32–33 Impact Craters

If your experiment worked, then the asteroid would have punched through the top layer and sent debris from this layer and the cocoa layer flying across the surface. Try dropping the asteroid from different heights and add more layers to your planet to see what happens.

Pages 40–41 Clues on the Surface

Lava flow caused by volcanic activity will cover craters. If one area of a planet has fewer craters than another area, it is likely that it is because it has had a lot of geological activity, such as volcanic eruptions. The Amazonis region of Mars has few craters. That tells us the area has had more geological activity than the Sinus Sabeus region, which has more craters.

$$d = \sqrt{(x_2 - x_1) + (y_2 - y_1)^2}$$

GLOSSARY

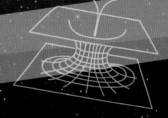

acid rain Rain with acidic components, such as sulfuric or nitric acid, which falls to the ground from the atmosphere.

artificial intelligence Intelligent behavior demonstrated by machines.

asteroids Large rocks found in the solar system.

atmosphere The blanket of gases around a planet.

canyon A deep, narrow valley with steep sides and often with a stream flowing through it.

carbon dioxide A gas humans breathe out which also occurs naturally.

comets Chunks of rock and ice in space, similar to asteroids.

constellations Shapes in the night sky formed by a pattern of stars.

data Facts and statistics.

debris The bits left after something has been destroyed.

descent Downward travel.

ejected Thrown out or off from inside.

erode To wear away by natural forces such as water and wind.

erosion When soil and rock are worn away by natural forces such as water and wind.

evaporates When a liquid turns into a gas.

far side of the moon The hemisphere, or half, of the moon that always faces away from Earth.

flyby The close approach of a spacecraft to a planet or moon for observation.

geologist A scientist who studies rocks and the surface and interior of Earth.

gravity The pull that any object has on any other. The bigger the object, or planet, the more gravity it has.

harvest To gather crops.

hostile Dangerous.

impact craters Holes in the surface of a planet or moon caused by an asteroid or comet strike.

infrared Invisible light emitted by heated objects.

lander A space probe that can land on a planet or moon and take measurements.

lava Hot, molten rock, which usually erupts from a volcano.

marsquakes The Martian versions of earthquakes.

meteorites Rocks from space that land on the ground.

microbes Tiny life forms, including germs, which can be seen only with a microscope.

nuclear weapons Explosive devices that get their force from nuclear reactions.

orbited Moved in a circular or oval path around another object in space, due to the pull of its gravity.

orbiter An unmanned spacecraft that flies in orbit around a planet for a long time to collect images and data.

ozone layer A layer in a planet's atmosphere that is made from ozone gas.

phases Changes in the moon's or a planet's shape as seen from Earth, caused by the changing position of the object in relation to the sun.

plate tectonics An explanation of the way large pieces of Earth's surface move.

pressure Pushing force.

probes Unmanned spacecraft designed for exploration.

radiation Energy in the form of waves or particles.

rocket A vehicle that burns fuel and oxygen to create thrust.

sample-return missions Missions in which samples are collected and returned to Earth so that they can be studied.

samples A small part or quantity of something that shows what the whole is like.

satellite An object that orbits a larger object. They can be natural, such as the moon, or human-made, such as an orbiter.

seismometer A machine that measures the shaking of the ground during a volcano or earthquake.

sensors Scientific devices that can detect a physical property and react to it.

solar system The sun, its planets and moons, asteroids, and comets.

Space Race The competition between the United States and the USSR that began with *Sputnik 1* in 1957 and ended when *Apollo 11* landed on the moon in 1969.

space shuttle A spacecraft that is designed to travel into space and back to Earth several times.

sulfuric acid A dangerous chemical that will burn through clothes, skin, and flesh.

summits The highest points of mountains.

tape recorder An old-fashioned device using tapes that store and play data.

telescopes Instruments shaped like long tubes that contain lenses inside them that make distant things seem larger and nearer when you look through the instrument.

topographic map A map that shows the different heights of a region. Red or brown areas are usually highest, while blue regions are lowest.

transmitters Devices that can send back information to a specific place.

ultraviolet (UV) Radiation with slightly shorter wavelengths than visible light. Naturally produced by the sun.

volcanoes Places where molten rock erupts onto the surface of a planet.

zodiac Ring of constellations around the whole sky that the sun, moon, and planets pass through.

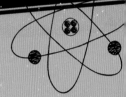

FURTHER READING

BOOKS

Carney, Elizabeth. *Mars* (National Geographic Kids: Level 3). Washington, D.C.: National Geographic Kids, 2014.

Dickmann, Nancy. *Exploring the Inner Planets* (Spectacular Space Science). New York, NY: Rosen Central, 2015.

Graham, Ian. *Planets Near Earth* (Space). Collingwood, ON: Smart Apple Media, 2015.

Sparrow, Giles. *Earth and the Inner Planets* (Space Travel Guides). Collingwood, ON: Smart Apple Media, 2011.

WEBSITES

Due to the changing nature of Internet links, PowerKids Press has developed an online list of websites related to the subject of this book. This site is updated regularly. Please use this link to access the list: **www.powerkidslinks.com/bass/nearestneighbors**

INDEX